Ocean Rescue

Written by Mary-Anne Creasy

Illustrated by Meredith Thomas

Flying Start
to Literacy®

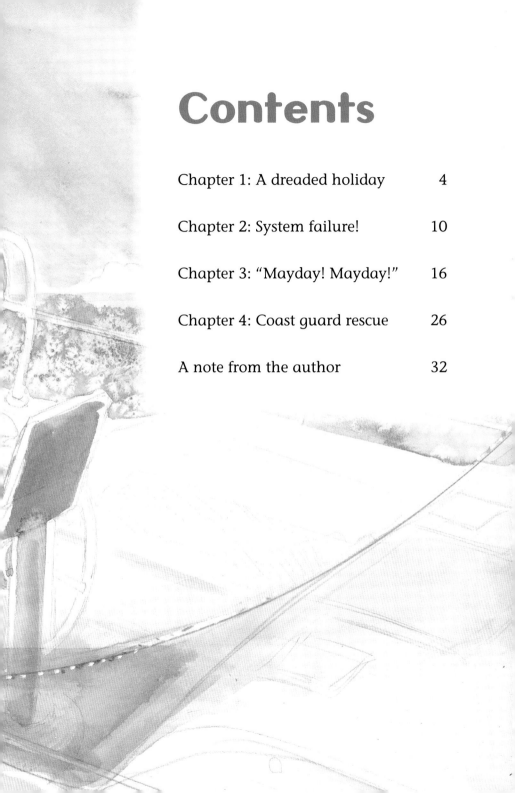

Contents

Chapter 1
A dreaded holiday

I have never liked the water. Even though I am a good swimmer, the thought of being out in the open ocean fills me with dread. So when Mum and Dad announced Grandpa was taking Sophie, Peter and me sailing for a week, I wasn't happy.

"Why can't I stay home?" I asked.

"You can't – sorry, Joe. Mum and I are going away for work," said Dad. "Grandpa used to take me sailing when I was little, and thought it would be fun if you kids had a sailing holiday."

Sophie and Peter were excited. Peter was only a year and a half older than me – he was fourteen. He couldn't wait to go snorkelling, and Sophie wanted to see a mermaid, but she was only eight.

Their excitement about the trip made my misery seem worse. "Mermaids aren't real, you know," I said, trying to dampen Sophie's happiness.

When we first got on Grandpa's boat, the *Nimbus*, I went straight down into the cabin. It was okay when we first set off, but when we got out into the open water and crossed the rough channel, the boat bobbed up and down as it ploughed through the waves.

I was scared. I was sure the boat was going to sink. And I felt seasick with the motion in the choppy waves. I climbed up onto the deck, pale and trembling.

Grandpa was steering through the rough seas. When he saw my grey face, he laughed. "Yep, it's better up on deck if you feel sick."

So I had to sit there in the wind and stare out at the sea, wishing I was back at home.

Grandpa showed Peter the GPS navigation system. "It's much better than maps because they constantly update the information. The only problem is, if the system goes down, then it's like sailing blind."

When Grandpa said that, it made me even more nervous. Every now and then, when no one was looking, I went up to make sure the GPS was still working.

We spent the whole week sailing. Sophie and Peter loved it; they leant over the sides as the *Nimbus* cut through the clear blue water. They jumped fearlessly into the ocean to swim and snorkel around the coral reefs.

At first, they tried to get me to go into the water: "Come on, Joe, there's nothing to be afraid of!" they called to me.

But I didn't like it. The ocean seemed bottomless and we were a long way from land. They quickly gave up and left me alone.

After a week at sea, we were at last heading home. Grandpa said we were going to sail the quick way back. He said it should take only five hours if the wind went the right way. By seven o'clock, we would be back onshore.

"Grandpa, can I steer the boat before we go out into the channel?" asked Peter.

"Sure," said Grandpa. He showed Peter the course on the GPS and where to steer.

"You're doing a great job," said Grandpa. "Stay on course. I'm going down below to help Joe and Sophie pack up."

We had nearly finished packing when Peter called out, "Grandpa! Something's wrong with the GPS. It says System Failure."

Grandpa dropped the bag he was holding, and we all rushed up to the deck. My stomach fluttered with fear.

Grandpa checked the switches and controls, but the GPS was definitely not working.

Chapter 2

System failure!

"Are we lost, Grandpa?" Sophie asked nervously.

Grandpa squeezed Sophie's hand. "No way, kiddo. It'll be okay. We've got some maps here – we've got radio communication. We'll be fine."

I looked at Grandpa's face, but he quickly turned away. He seemed worried.

"Peter, can you radio in to the coast guard and let them know what's happening?" asked Grandpa. "I'm going to find those maps."

Peter switched on the radio and pressed the button on the microphone as Grandpa had shown all three of us to do in an emergency. There was nothing but static.

Grandpa came up onto the deck holding some rolled-up maps. "Anything?" he asked. Peter shook his head.

Grandpa took the microphone, pressed the Call button and tried again. Still nothing. "We'll keep trying," he said.

He unrolled the maps on the table and pointed to a spot on one of them. "I think we're about here, and it looks like we've got a clear passage between these two islands – so we'll keep steering this way. Then once we get past, we'll be on our way."

A cold gust of wind blew up and the sails filled with
air. Grandpa steered the *Nimbus* as we
raced towards the open sea. Then, just as
suddenly, the wind dropped and blew
from the other direction.

"Everybody hang on!" yelled Grandpa as the boom
swung around to the other side and the boat
tipped to one side. We held on tight as spray
from the waves splashed our faces.

Grandpa and Peter quickly wound down the mainsail. Without so much sail to catch the wind, the boat slowed down.

"Okay, I want everyone in wet-weather gear and life jackets. NOW! Let's get everything ready in case the wind picks up again," said Grandpa, eyeing the looming dark clouds.

I ran to the locker where the life jackets were stowed and handed one out to everyone. Soon, we were warmer and I felt safer with my life jacket on.

"Are we going to be all right?" I asked Grandpa.

"Yeah, sure – we'll be fine. We've just got to get past these islands and into the deep channel. This is the most dangerous part because of the reef, and there are some wrecks here, too."

Suddenly, there was a grinding noise from below us and I felt the boat shudder.

"What's that noise?" I yelled.

"I think we've hit something. I'm going to swim under the boat and check it out," said Grandpa. He grabbed his mask and snorkel, and then pulled off his jacket.

We watched as Grandpa, wearing his mask and flippers, disappeared over the side.

Sophie started to cry. "I want to go home."

I wanted to be off the *Nimbus* and safe at home, too, but I didn't want to scare Sophie by saying that.

"What if we sink, Peter?" I asked in a low voice so Sophie couldn't hear me, but she did.

"*Sink? Are we going to sink?*"

Peter pressed his lips together and glared at me. "No, we're not going to sink. Everything is okay."

But he looked nervous.

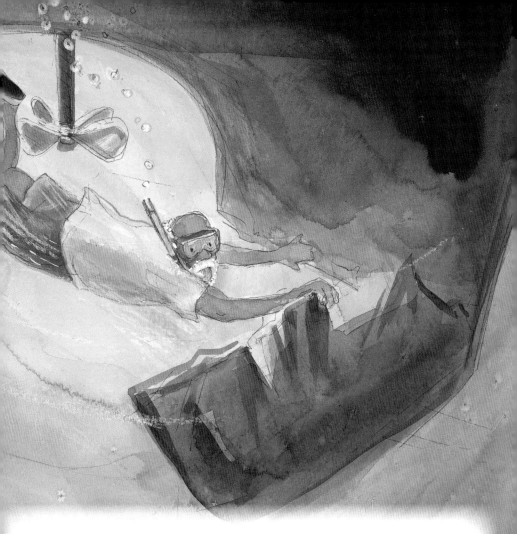

Grandpa finally surfaced and climbed onto the deck. He looked worried. "Yeah, it's not good, kids. The keel has broken."

"*The keel?*" Peter asked. "Is that the long thing under the boat that helps keep it from tipping over?"

"Yeah." Grandpa nodded. "We're going to have to prepare to abandon ship."

Chapter 3

"Mayday! Mayday!"

Grandpa gathered us around him. "All right, I want everyone to get ready. At the moment, we're okay – but if the wind picks up, the *Nimbus* might tip over. We're going to have to get into the life raft fast, so do everything I say. Do it calmly and we'll be fine."

Just then, a gust of wind blew and the boat began to shift at an angle. Sophie screamed and stumbled. She began to cry. Peter reached out and grabbed her.

Grandpa pointed to the front of the boat. "Peter, go to the locker and get the life raft. It's in the heavy orange plastic bag."

Then he turned to Sophie and cradled her. "Sophie, sit on the deck. See this radio? I want you to press this button and say 'Mayday! Mayday!' Then wait. If you hear anyone reply, let me know."

Sophie wiped the tears from her face and tried to look brave. "Okay," she nodded.

As Grandpa put on his life jacket, he turned to me. "Joe, go below and grab as many water bottles as you can carry. And be quick!"

My head was spinning and my heart was beating fast. Down in the cabin, I frantically grabbed some bottles and filled them with water.

I felt a lump in my throat. I wanted to go back up on deck; it wasn't safe down below. What if the *Nimbus* started sinking? I could feel the waves pushing against the boat as I stumbled in the kitchen, opening cupboards while searching for a bag.

I found a plastic bag and quickly shoved in the bottles of water. The boat began to tilt and I dragged myself up the steps.

As I went back onto the deck, Grandpa was holding something in his hand. It looked like a water bottle with an antenna sticking out.

"What's that?" I asked.

"This is an emergency beacon," Grandpa said. "It sends a signal of our location to satellites in space. The signal is transmitted to the coast guard. The coast guard will be able to see where we are and send help."

"How long will it take to rescue us? Will they come
right away?"

Grandpa nodded. "Yep, they'll be here right away." He
switched on the beacon and it began to flash. He put it in
a compartment where it would be visible and turned to help
Peter. A gust of wind pushed the waves higher and the boat
tilted even more.

"Okay, guys, we're going off the back of the boat."

Grandpa tied the orange bag to a metal loop on the back of the boat. He threw the bag into the water and then yanked on the cord that dangled from it. The bag burst open and filled with air. In seconds, it had become a small life raft, complete with a tent for cover. He dragged it closer to the *Nimbus* and threw the bag of water bottles inside.

"All right, Peter, I want you to go in first so you can help the other two."

Peter nodded. He pushed off from the boat, falling through the opening of the tent. "Ow!" he yelled.

"Are you okay?" asked Grandpa.

"Yeah," Peter said. "My arm just landed funny on top
of the water bottles."

The choppy waves made the life raft hit the *Nimbus* and
Grandpa pushed it away with his foot. He shouted to
Peter, "I'm going to have to let the life raft drift away
a bit! I don't want it to get damaged by the boat."

Peter looked out, fearful, as Grandpa loosened the rope
and Peter floated further away.

"Okay, Joe, you're next," said Grandpa.

I looked down at the water. It was rough now, and I imagined the waves crashing over me and pushing me down. I shook my head.

"I can't jump that far!" I said.

"No, Joe, you're going to have to swim," said Grandpa. "It's not far – only a few metres."

"Joe, please go – I'm scared!" said Sophie. She was crying and hugging Grandpa.

I stood on the step and the water washed up over my feet. I knew I didn't have a choice. The life raft didn't look that far away.

"Jump, then swim!" yelled Grandpa.

I held my breath and jumped. I waited for my head to go under, but it didn't. The life jacket held me up out of the water and I bobbed around for a few seconds.

Peter leaned forward and shouted, "Swim, Joe, swim!"

It was hard to swim wearing the life jacket. When I got close
enough, Peter reached down with one arm to help me.

I flopped into the raft, panting with fear.

"You did it – you're safe!" said Peter as he hugged me close.

I noticed Peter was clutching his arm. "What happened? Are you okay?" I asked.

"Nothing. I just landed funny on my arm," said Peter, but he gripped his wrist and looked pale.

Before I could say anything, Grandpa yelled, "Okay, guys, I'm going to pull the life raft in so Sophie doesn't have to swim so far."

Peter yelled, "You'll be fine, Sophie. It's easy, and you're a good swimmer!"

Sophie nodded but looked scared. Grandpa started to search his pockets.

"Kids, I forgot the emergency beacon!" He looked down at Sophie. "It's okay – I won't be long. Just hang on."

Grandpa clambered up the back of the *Nimbus* while Sophie held on to the metal railing.

The weather grew wilder, the wind stronger and the waves higher. A huge wave slapped one side of the boat. We watched helplessly as the boat tipped on its side. Sophie screamed as she plunged into the water.

Chapter 4

Coast guard rescue

"Peter, help!" Sophie yelled, and she began to swim clumsily towards us in her life jacket, though she wasn't getting closer.

"Peter, you have to go in and help her," I said urgently.

Peter shook his head. "I can't – it's my wrist. It might be broken. You'll have to go in."

"Joe, please help me!" yelled Sophie.

I leant down, looking at the water. It was rough. Then I saw Sophie's frightened face.

"Okay, don't worry – I'm coming!" I jumped into the water and swam over to Sophie. Waves slapped over us and I had to spit out water. But at last, we reached the life raft. I helped Sophie in and then Peter used his good arm to pull her up.

Our life raft was still tied to the *Nimbus* and the rope
was pulled tight. If the boat started sinking, it would
pull us under.

"We have to untie the rope!" said Peter. "Joe, you have
to do it!"

I swam back to the boat and untied the rope. Immediately,
we drifted further away.

"Grandpa!" I yelled, but there was no answer. "I have to
find him!" I began to swim around the back of the *Nimbus*.

"Joe, what are you doing?" cried Peter. "Get back in the
life raft – we can paddle around."

Just then, we saw Grandpa swimming towards us from the other side of the boat.

"Grandpa, over here!" we yelled.

Grandpa waved, then slowly made his way over to us.

"It's okay, Grandpa, I've got you," I said, reaching out to grab his life jacket.

"You sure do, Joe – thanks for that!" Grandpa said as I helped him into the life raft.

"I was getting the beacon when the *Nimbus* tipped over and I fell into the water on the other side!" Grandpa said, panting. He hugged us all. "We made it! Good job, kids."

Then I noticed the emergency beacon tied to Grandpa's life jacket. "Grandpa, do you think it worked? Do you think the coast guard will come soon?"

"It's sure to work," said Grandpa. "But we might have a long wait. At least we're safe now."

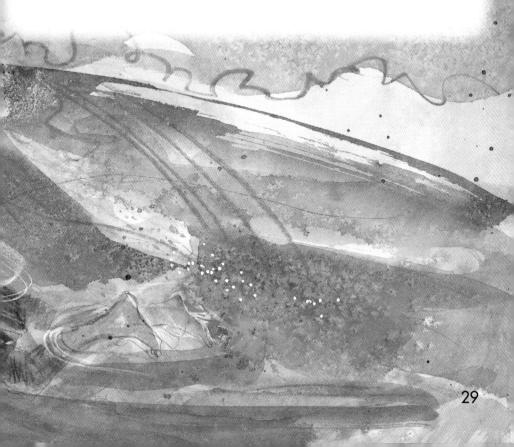

We spent the next several hours drifting in the small life raft, carefully sipping the bottled water. The wind gradually died down and the ocean became calm. The clouds disappeared, and the stars and the moon came out once it grew dark.

Finally, sometime after midnight, we saw a speck of light in the distance. It slowly grew larger and we could hear the rumble of a boat's engine. We also heard a voice blaring through a loudspeaker.

"Coast guard to *Nimbus* crew, prepare for rescue!"

We were saved!

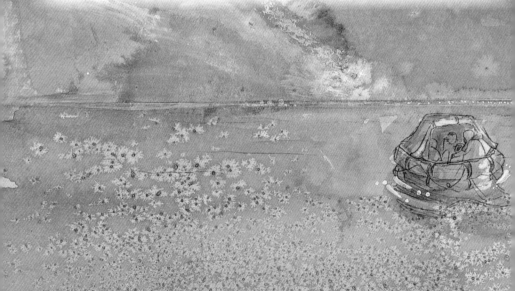

Far above us, among the stars, was a satellite that had received our signal and sent it on to the coast guard for our emergency rescue. That signal had saved our lives.

As the coast guard vessel got closer, its big searchlight shone brightly in our eyes. The engine switched off, and one of the crew members climbed down a ladder and leant out with a long stick to pull our life raft closer to the boat.

"Hey, kids, who wants to get off first?" she asked.

"We're safe now, kids!" said Grandpa, once we were on the coast guard boat, and he hugged all three of us tightly. "You were fantastic, Joe, so brave! You're not afraid of the ocean anymore, are you?"

I smiled at Grandpa and shook my head. "No, not at all."

Then suddenly, a wave slapped against the boat. I lurched sideways and gasped, gripping Peter's arm.

"Well, maybe a little," I admitted.

A note from the author

When I did research for this book, I spent a long time on the Internet watching videos of people who live on yachts and sail long distances all over the world. Some kids are even raised on boats, learning to sail and learning to live in a tiny house on the water.

It looked like fun, but sometimes it must be scary, especially when there is a storm or they hit something in the water. Kids have to learn what to do in an emergency, because when something goes wrong everybody has to help.